F

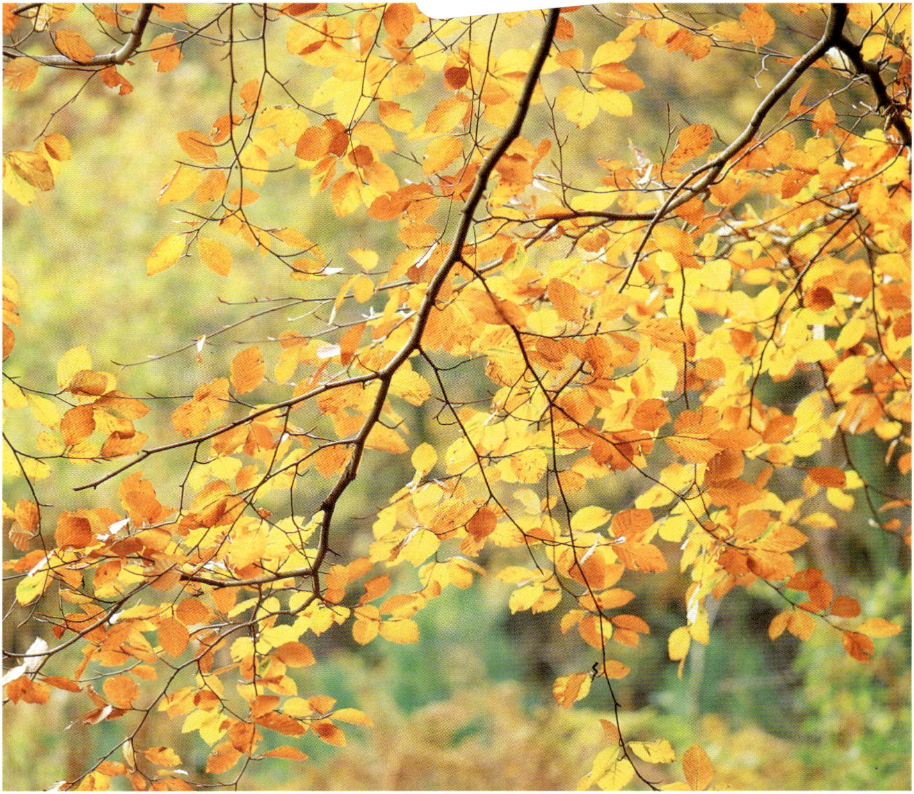

Judy Nayer

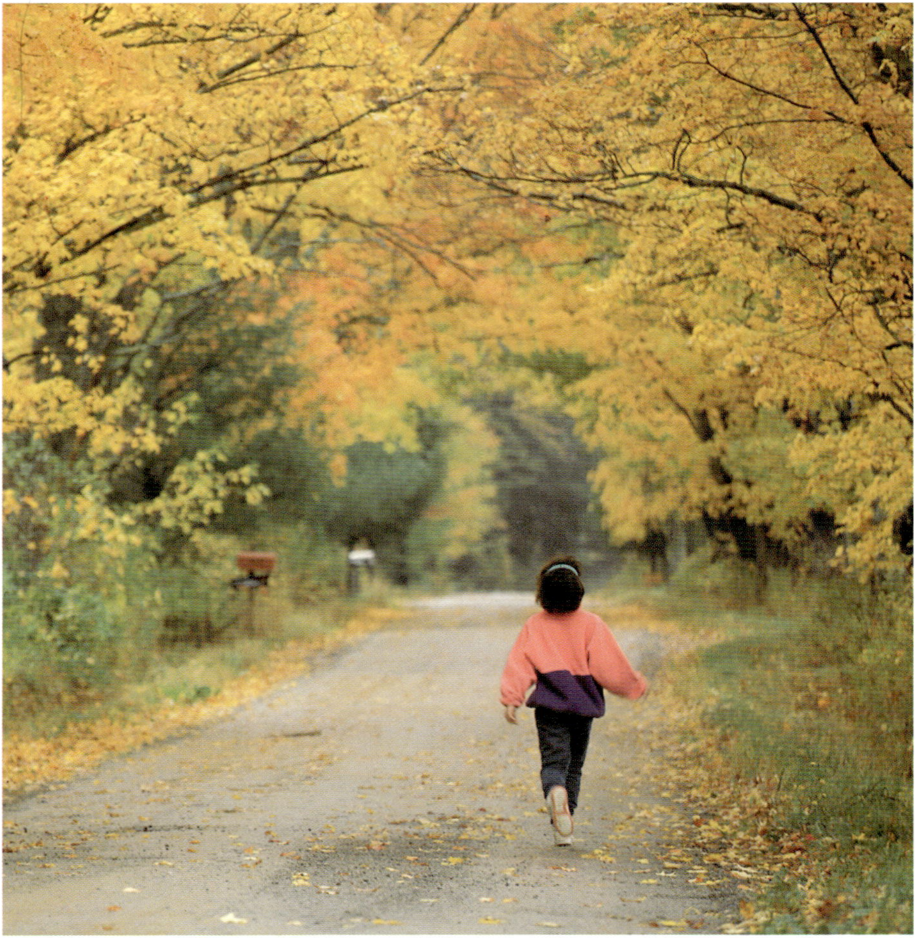

Fall is leaves,

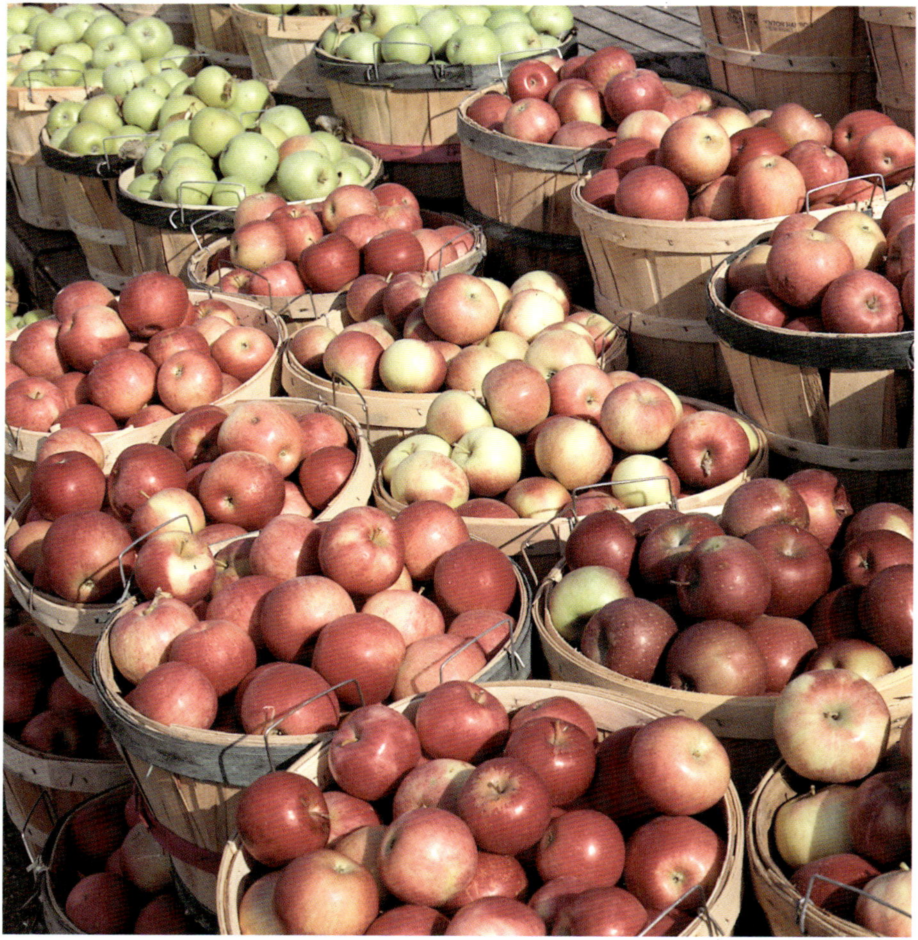

apples,

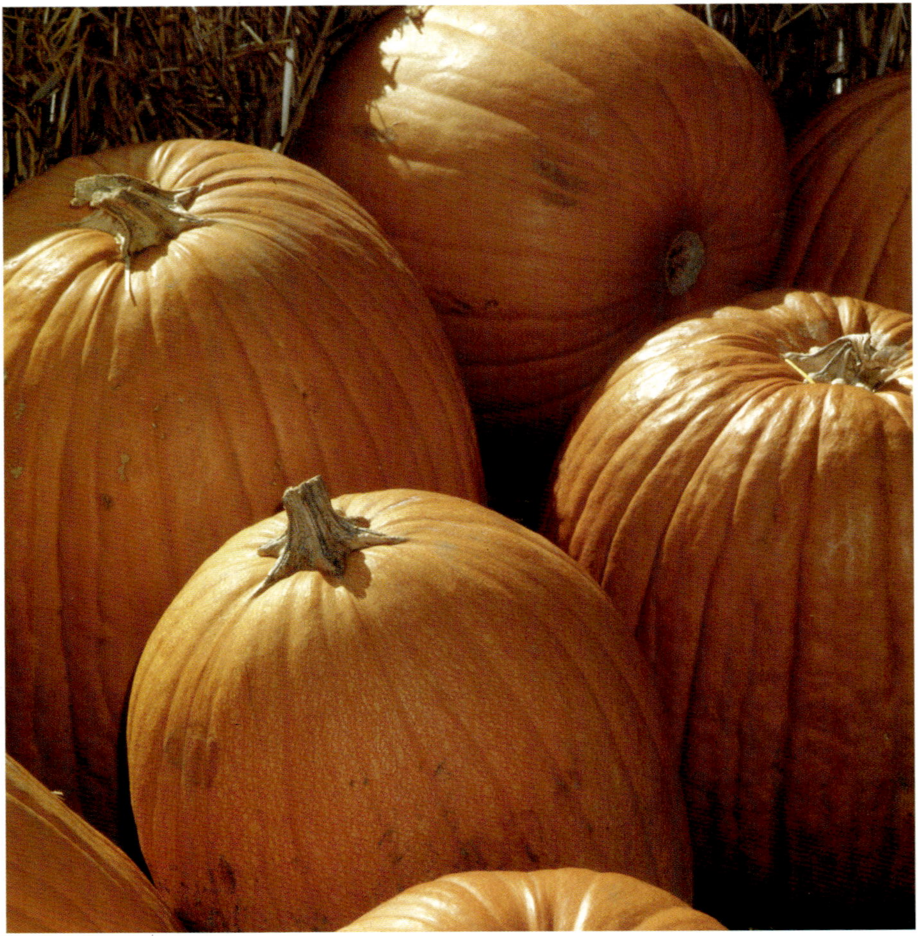

pumpkins,

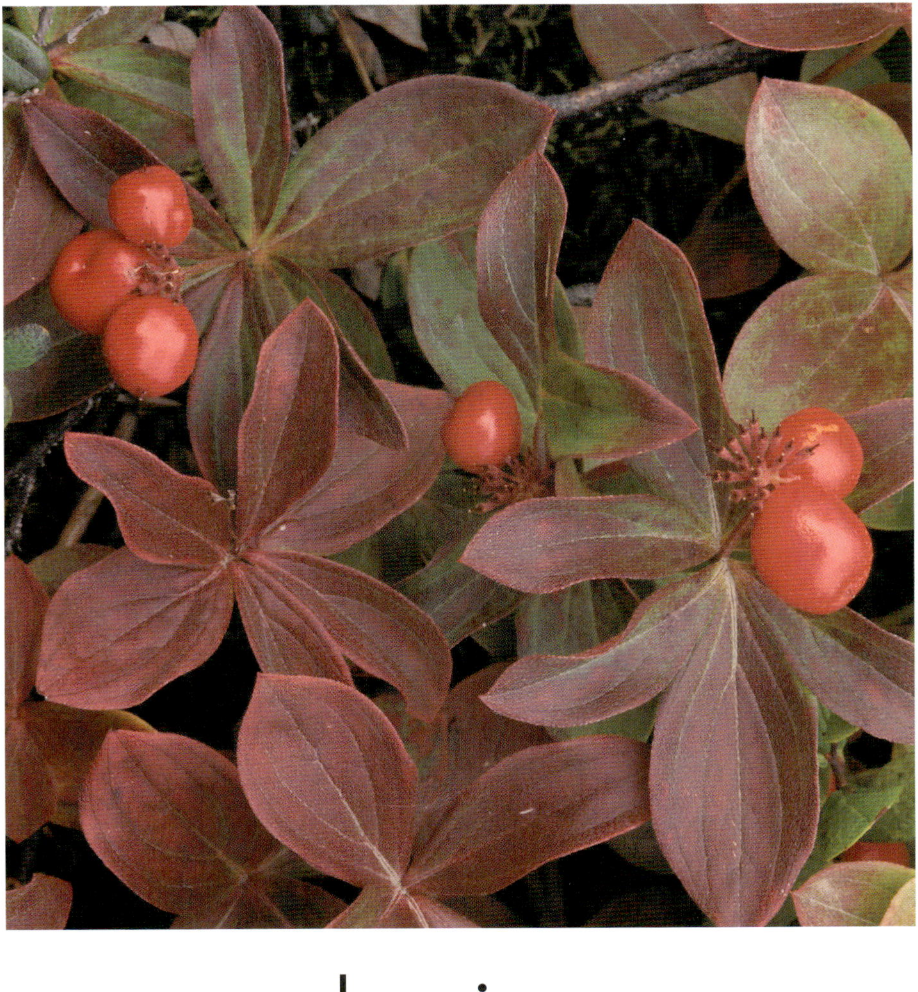

berries,

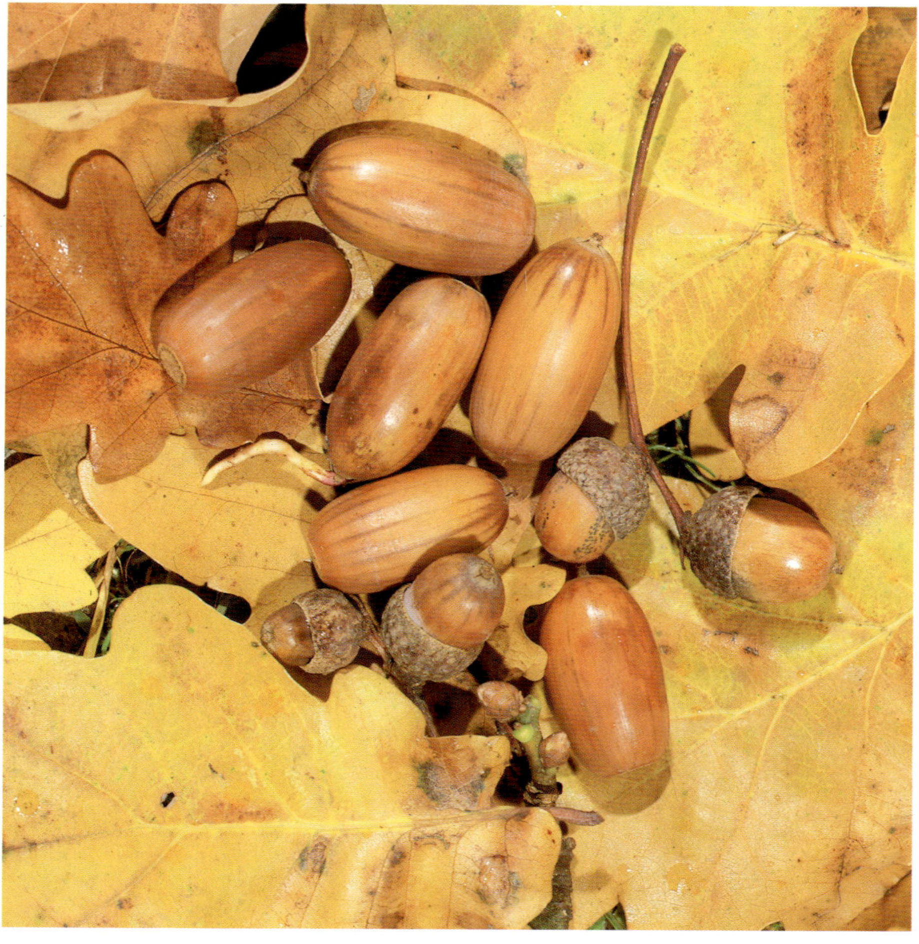

acorns,

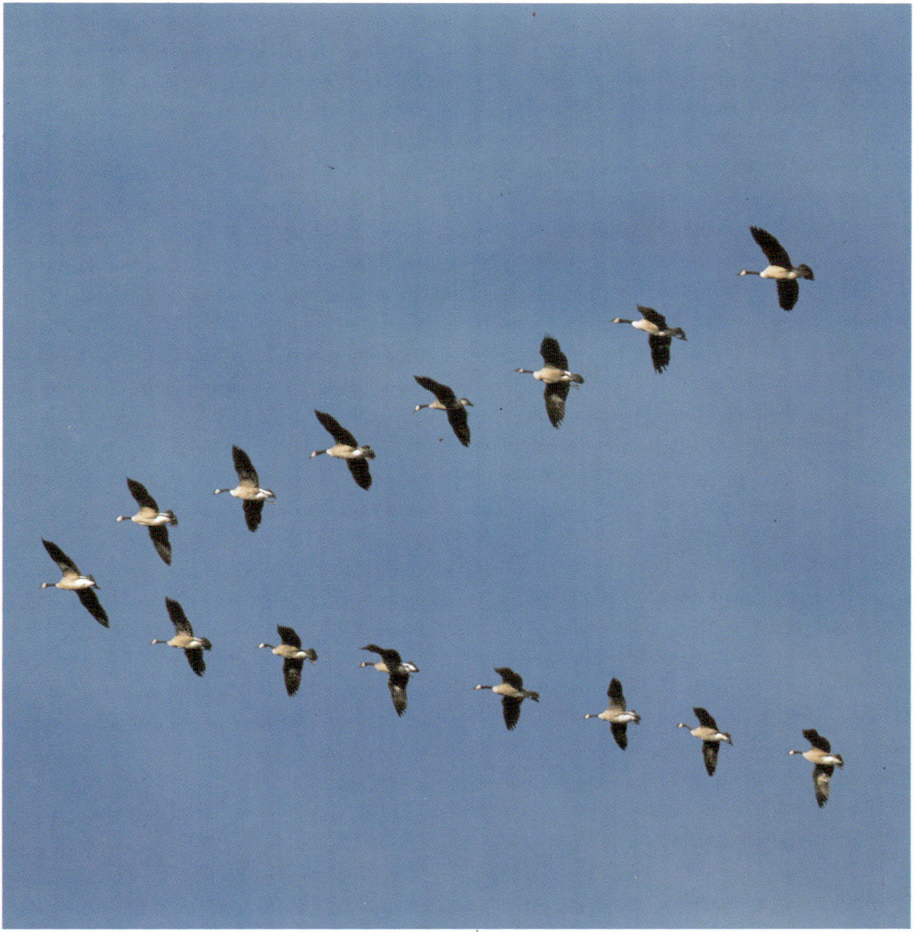

and geese.

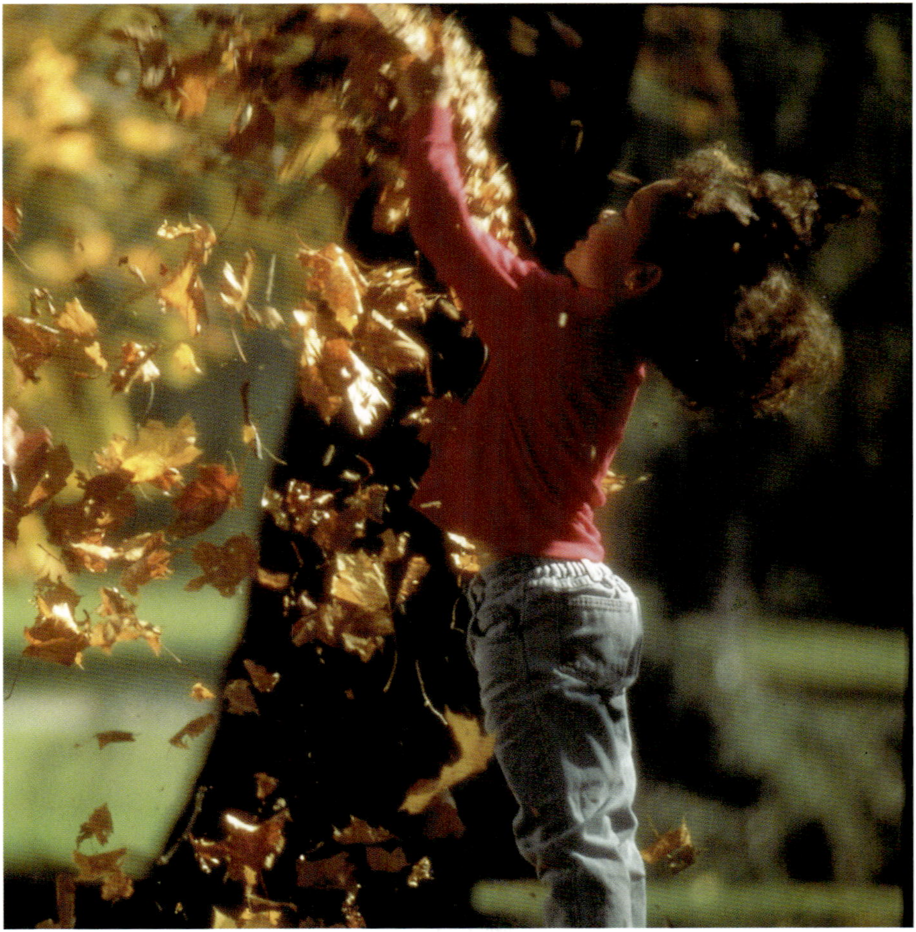

Fall is fun!